TOTTERING-BY-GENTLY®

HE TALKS MARS

ANNIE TEMPEST

F

FRANCES LINCOLN LIMITED
PUBLISHERS

Frances Lincoln Limited
4 Torriano Mews
Torriano Avenue
London NW5 2RZ
www.franceslincoln.com

She Talks Venus, He Talks Mars
Copyright © The O'Shea Gallery 2011
Text copyright © Annie Tempest 2011
Illustrations copyright © Annie Tempest 2011

British Library Cataloguing in Publication Data
A catalogue record for this book is available from the British Library.

ISBN 978-0-7112-3261-7

Printed in China
Bound for North Pimmshire

9 8 7 6 5 4 3 2 1

Other Tottering-by-Gently books by Annie Tempest:
Out and About with the Totterings
Drinks with the Totterings
In the Garden with the Totterings
The Totterings' Desk Diary
The Totterings' Pocket Diary
Tottering-by-Gently Annual
Available from Frances Lincoln at www.franceslincoln.com

At Home with the Totterings
Tottering-by-Gently Vol III
Available from The Tottering Drawing Room, along with a full range of Tottering-by-Gently licensed product, at The O'Shea Gallery, No. 4 St James's Street, London SW1A 1EF (Telephone +44 (0)207 930 5880) or www.tottering.com

THE O'SHEA GALLERY

Raymond O'Shea of The O'Shea Gallery was originally one of London's leading antiquarian print and map dealers. Historically, antiquarian galleries sponsored and promoted contemporary artists who they felt complemented their recognized areas of specialization. It was in this tradition that O'Shea first contacted *Country Life* magazine to see if Annie Tempest would like to be represented and sponsored by his gallery. In 1995 Raymond was appointed agent for Annie Tempest's originals and publisher of her books. Raymond is responsible for creating an archive of all of Annie's cartoons.

In 2003, the antiquarian side of his business was put on hold and the St. James's Street premises were finally converted to The Tottering Drawing Room at The O'Shea Gallery. It is now the flagship of a worldwide operation that syndicates and licenses illustrated books, prints, stationery, champagne, jigsaws, greetings cards, ties and much more. It has even launched its own fashion range of tweeds and shooting accessories under the label Gently Ltd.

The Tottering Drawing Room at The O'Shea Gallery is a wonderful location which is now available for corporate events of 45–125 people and is regularly used for private dinner parties catering for up to 14 people. Adjacent to St. James's Palace, the gallery lies between two famous 18th century shops: Berry Bros. & Rudd, the wine merchants and Locks, the hatters. Accessed through French doors at the rear of the gallery lies Pickering Place – not only the smallest public square in Great Britain, with original gas lighting, but it was also where the last duel in England was fought. A plaque on the wall, erected by the Anglo-Texan Society, indicates that from 1842–45 a building here was occupied by the Legation from the Republic of Texas to the Court of St. James.

Raymond O'Shea and Annie Tempest are delighted to be able to extend Tottering fans a warm welcome in the heart of historic St. James's where all the original Tottering watercolours can be seen along side a full product and print range.

'Arguing with a woman is like trying to fold the airmail edition of THE TIMES in a high wind.'

LORD MANCROFT

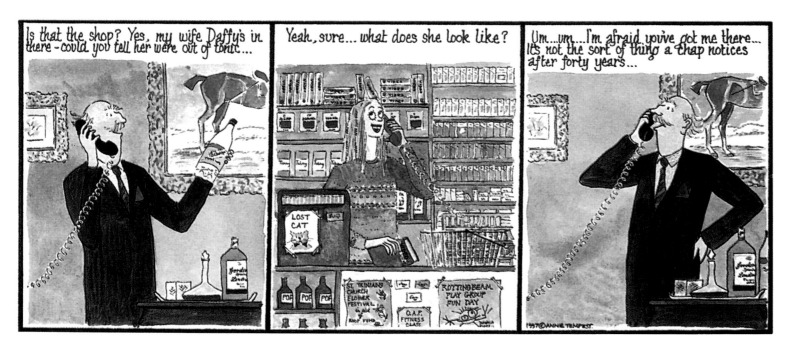

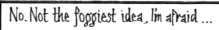

I'm turning into an amorphous lump on top of skinny legs -

Most men would take that as a cue to pay their wife a much needed compliment..

Your eyesight is excellent, dear...

Annie Tempest © 2009

No, no - tell me, darling - you know I'm always dying to hear all about what ever you've been up to in the garden...

My son has invited me out there but I can't go, you see, because of my dogs..

Then he says - 'who's more important - the dogs or your own grandchildren?'..

I hope you told him...

ANNIE TEMPEST ©2008

What's your PIN number, Darling?

You don't need a PIN number - it's a microwave oven...

How do you get the hot soup out then?..

Yes. Could you send a piano tuner out— I'm afraid a decanter of port got knocked into it...

Dicky! They need some details—age, make and so forth...

It was a 1928 Cockburn that my father put down for me...

" My quack tells me there's nothing he can give me to stop me having any more grandchildren..."

The bounder has fled North Pimmshire – clearly didn't know the Country Code...

You can get away with stealing another man's wife...

... but never his pheasants...

' Let's look on the bright side - at least we'll never have to hear "I told you so..." '

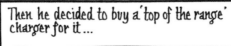

It's amazing how big birthdays bring on odd behaviour in men – Dicky suddenly decided he needed a BlackBerry...

Then he decided to buy a 'top of the range' charger for it...

...this is what he came back with...

" *You look fine as you are - now come down - we're leaving...* "

Lost her handbag... forgot to kiss the dog goodbye...five past eight...

...got to quickly ring so-and-so... left her lipstick upstairs...

ANNIE TEMPEST © 2005

I'd better go now... Dicky will be champing at the bit downstairs...

The trouble with being punctual for one's wife is that she's never there to appreciate it...

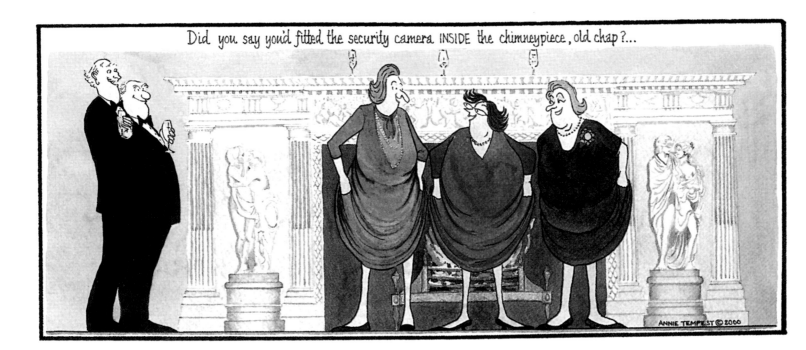

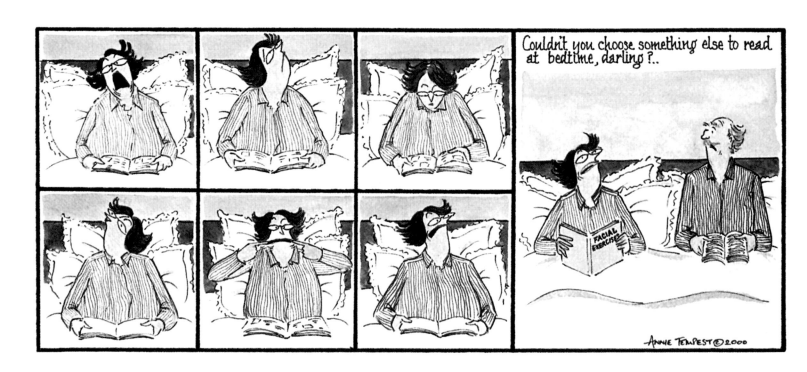

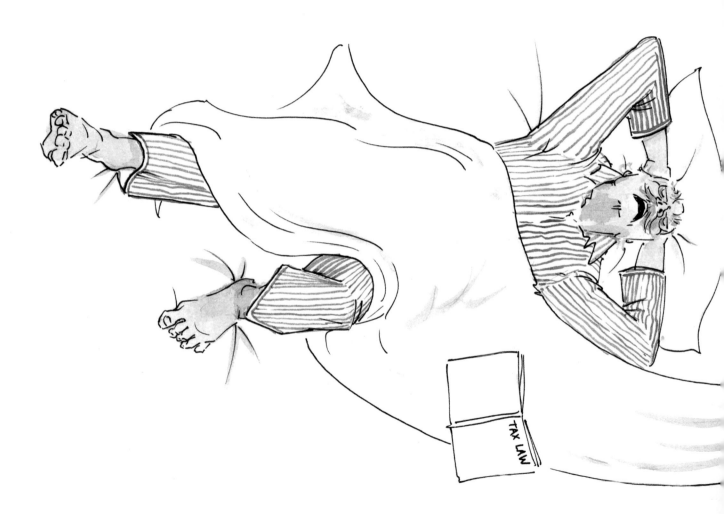

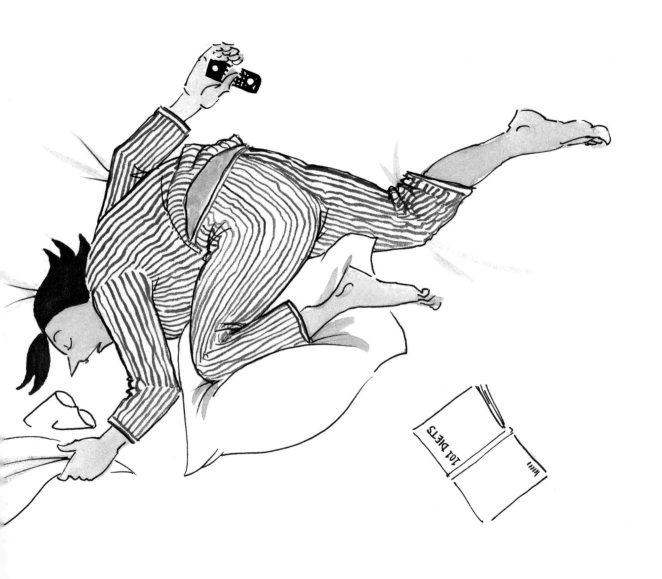

I'm stapel-gunning the bedclothes down to my side of the bed ...

Just sorting out a problem that communication has failed to remedy ...

What on earth are you doing, Daffy?

THE MARRIED WOMAN: A tendency to forget what a romantic gesture looks like...

For Heaven's sake! Someone's chucked Orchids and Peonies all over my bed! Just look at that MESS!

Happy Birthday, Darling...

Yup - it's that way. I remember passing
that tree that looks like a T.Rex in an
Ascot hat...

Just don't rush me - it's coming back
to me...

Of course we're not lost, Dicky - I told you-
I'll remember the way as we go along...

Do I look all right, Dicky?

Fine - yes, lovely... why?

Just testing a theory...

" I know I said I was only going to look but it's a woman's prerogative to change her mind, darling..."

ANNIE TEMPEST '97

'Mine's a Gin and Tonic...'

'Mine's a Holland and Holland...'

'Mine's a Grant and Lang...'

Men have been hunter-gatherers since time immemorial and they're still at it ...
Thankyou, dear...
Annie Tempest © 2008
Shame that women have evolved out of thinking that a brace of dead birds is a nice present...

...on the sofa with a large glass of wine and a pile of mail order catalogues...

I couldn't agree more, Dicky...

A woman's place should be in the home...

Daffy! What on earth are you doing! That's the second red light we've gone straight through!

Sorry, darling – I was just distracted for a second listening to woman's hour...

...I thought you were driving...

... recycle our household waste ....

Oh! Well done! I suppose it's what the government's encouraging us all to do ....

My husband ran off with another woman so I divorced him ... she's welcome to him.

After one large gin and tonic Dicky is quite
charming and amusing...

After two or three he starts becoming a bit
of a bore...

...and if I have a fourth, I just keel over,
fall asleep and snore loudly...

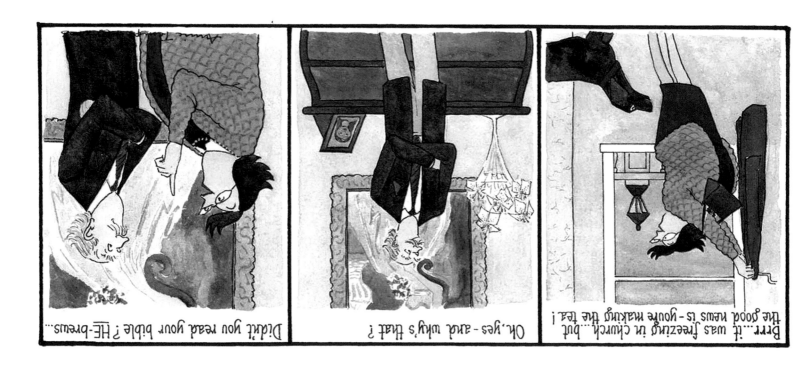

Yikes! It's cold! My hands are frozen stiff...

Why didn't you wear the lovely gloves I gave you for Christmas?

Because I don't want to lose them...

"...sitting timing how many hours I'm getting per light bulb?"

"Women don't go in for pointless arithmatic like that... I mean where would it end?..."

"If you don't zero your mileometer after filling up how are you going to work out how many miles you're getting to the gallon..."

"...and don't you go getting any funny ideas – I only bought it so I could shout into your good ear..."

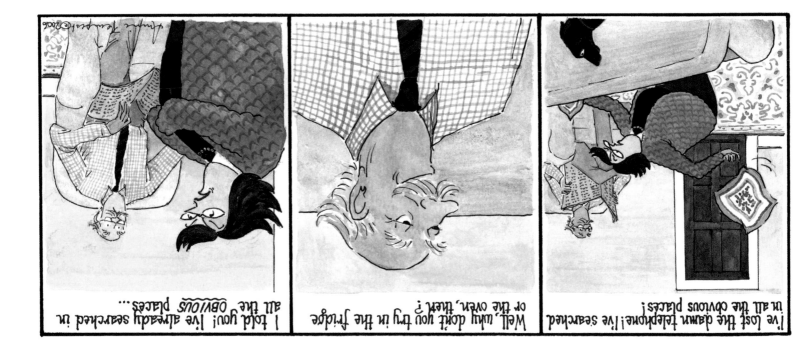

That man was incredibly rude to you!

Oh! Don't worry - I've dealt with it - he's on the same local flight as you...

...and I've sent his luggage to Nairobi.

Oh! Give it here! I know exactly where it is - its in blue biro by the coffee stain on the inside cover...

...or under 'E' for Ernie... its not under 'M' for mole man - I've even tried 'U' for useful garden people...

I can't find Ernie Dagless's number in your telephone book, Daffy - its not under 'D' for Dagless...

A raquort forks not quite in the same league, Dicky...

What?! How can you say that, Daffy? Only last week I bought you a lovely present...

Oh! It's beautiful! You're so lucky - Dicky never buys me presents these days...

ANNIE TEMPEST '06

THE FEMALE ART OF DENIAL : These aren't wrinkles – they're characterful laughter lines...

"You may well be in your cave on Mars but
the children and I are still living here
in North Finmshire..."

Well, darling - you've just got to communicate
with him - say it to him as it is...

I'm fed up with him being so distant...he's
never really there for us...

No, Dicky— I'm trying to explain the male ego ...

Not still going on about that lace night dress you want for Christmas, are you?...

Well, it's rather like that 'soldier' vase— massive but very delicate ...

I'm going too to one on the Louis Mariette hat romping straight to the front page of HELLO! Magazine...

Which one are you backing, darling?

Ooh! I love Ladies day!...

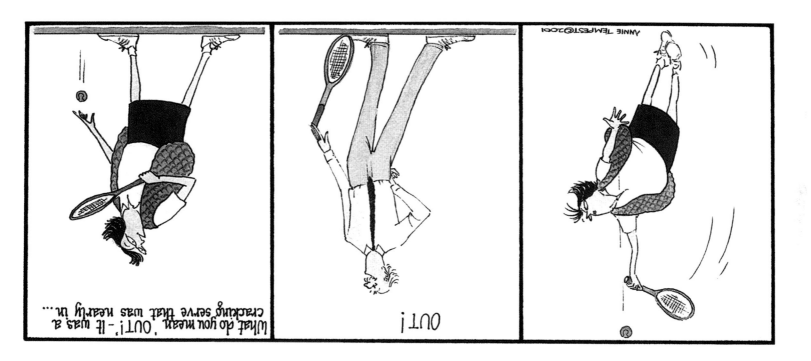

What do you mean, 'OUT!' - It was a cracking serve that was nearly in....

OUT!

ANNIE TEMPEST©2001

"I'm afraid it's just a characteristic of the breed – Let them off the leash for two minutes and they run away to their club and drink too much..."

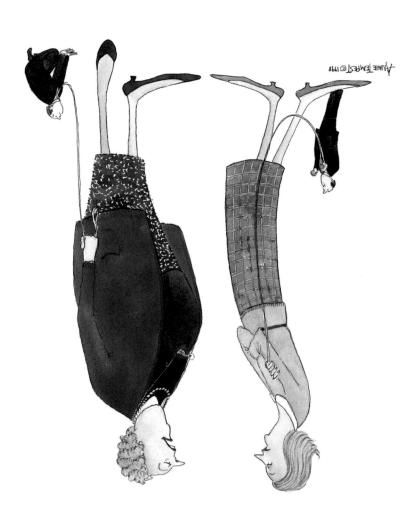

Annie Tempest © 1998

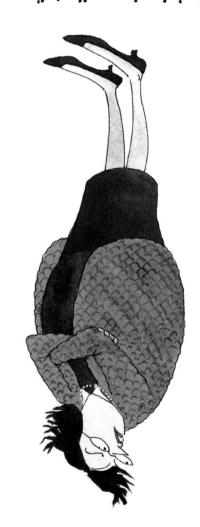

"... and what makes you think I'm angry?"

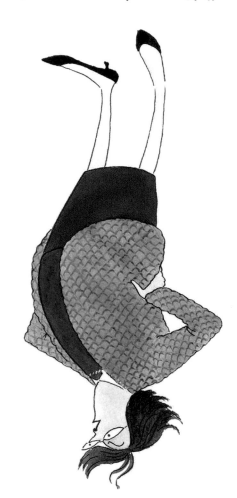

"You can't blame my hormones every time—this time you'll just have to make an effort to accept you're in the wrong."

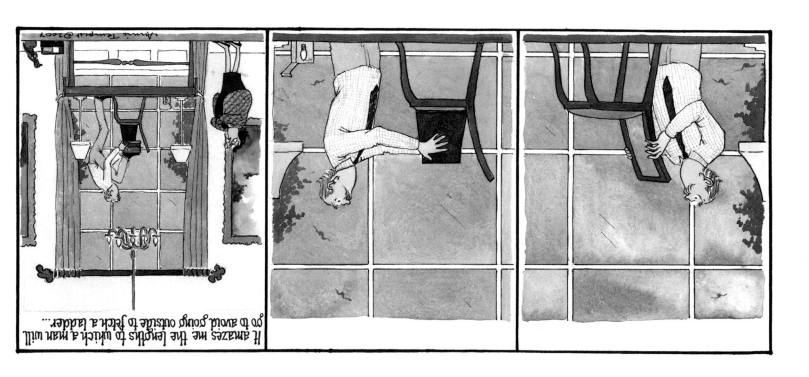

It amazes me the lengths to which a man will go to avoid going outside to fetch a ladder...

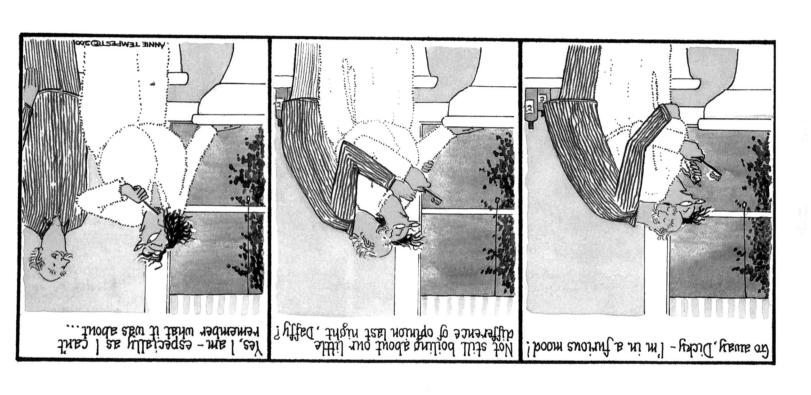

TOTTERING-BY-GENTLY ®
ANNIE TEMPEST

Annie Tempest is one of the top cartoonists working in the UK. This was recognized in 2009 when the Cartoon Art Trust awarded her the prestigious Pont Prize for the portrayal of the British Character.

Annie's cartoon career began in 1985 with the success of her first book, *How Green Are Your Wellies?* This led to a regular cartoon, 'Westenders' in the *Daily Express*. Soon after, she joined the *Daily Mail* with 'The Yuppies' cartoon strip which ran for more than seven years and for which, in 1989, she was awarded 'Strip Cartoonist of the Year'. Since 1993 Annie Tempest has been charting the life of Daffy and Dicky Tottering in Tottering-by-Gently – the phenomenally successful weekly strip cartoon in *Country Life* magazine.

Daffy Tottering is a woman of a certain age who has been taken into the hearts of people all over the world. She reflects the problems facing women in their everyday life and is completely at one with herself, while reflecting on the intergenerational tensions and the differing perspectives of men and women, as well as dieting, ageing, gardening, fashion, food, field sports, convention and much more.

Daffy and her husband Dicky live in the fading grandeur of Tottering Hall, their stately home in the fictional county of North Pimmshire, with their extended family: son and heir Hon Jon, daughter Serena, and grandchildren, Freddy and Daisy. The daily, Mrs Shagpile, and love of Dicky's life, Slobber, his black Labrador, and the latest addition to the family, Scribble, Daisy's working Cocker Spaniel, also make regular appearances.

Annie Tempest was born in Zambia in 1959. She has a huge international following and has had eighteen one-woman shows, from Mexico to Mayfair. Her work is now syndicated from New York to Dubai and she has had numerous collections of her cartoons published. *She Talks Venus He Talks Mars* is the latest to be published.

Frances Lincoln Limited
4 Torriano Mews
Torriano Avenue
London NW5 2RZ
www.franceslincoln.com

British Library Cataloguing in Publication Data
A catalogue record for this book is available from the British Library.

ISBN 978-0-7112-3261-7

Printed in China
Bound for North Pimmshire

9 8 7 6 5 4 3 2 1

Other Tottering-by-Gently books by Annie Tempest:
Out and About with the Totterings
Drinks with the Totterings
In the Garden with the Totterings
The Totterings' Desk Diary
The Totterings' Pocket Diary
Tottering-by-Gently Annual
Available from Frances Lincoln at www.franceslincoln.com

At Home with the Totterings
Tottering-by-Gently Vol III
Available from The Tottering Drawing Room, along with a full range of Tottering-by-Gently licensed product, at The O'Shea Gallery, No. 4 St James's Street, London SW1A 1EF (Telephone +44 (0)207 930 5880) or www.tottering.com

SHE TALKS VENUS

ANNIE TEMPEST

F

FRANCES LINCOLN LIMITED

PUBLISHERS

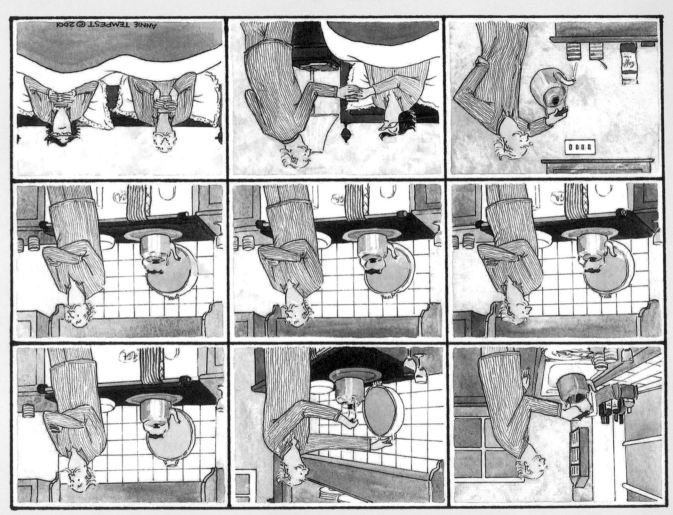

ANNIE TEMPEST © 2001